Mythical Creatures

DRAGONS

Martha London

DiscoverRoo
An Imprint of Pop!
popbooksonline.com

abdobooks.com

Published by Pop!, a division of ABDO, PO Box 398166, Minneapolis, Minnesota 55439.

Printed in the United States of America, North Mankato, Minnesota.

102019
012020

THIS BOOK CONTAINS RECYCLED MATERIALS

Cover Photo: Shutterstock Images
Interior Photos: Shutterstock Images, 1, 5, 16 (top), 16 (bottom left), 17 (top), 17 (bottom), 23 (left), 26–27, 28; iStockphoto, 6, 7, 9, 10, 11, 12–13, 14, 15, 19, 20, 21, 22, 23 (right), 25, 29, 30, 31; Chronicle/Alamy, 16 (bottom right)

Editor: Sophie Geister-Jones
Series Designer: Jake Nordby

Library of Congress Control Number: 2019942469

Publisher's Cataloging-in-Publication Data

Names: London, Martha, author.

Title: Dragons / by Martha London

Description: Minneapolis, Minnesota : Pop!, 2020 | Series: Mythical creatures | Includes online resources and index.

Identifiers: ISBN 9781532165740 (lib. bdg.) | ISBN 9781532167065 (ebook)

Subjects: LCSH: Mythical animals--Juvenile literature. | Dragons--Juvenile literature. | Folklore--Juvenile literature. | Legends--Juvenile literature. | Animals and history--Juvenile literature.

Classification: DDC 398.469--dc23

Pop open this book and you'll find QR codes loaded with information, so you can learn even more!

Scan this code* and others like it while you read, or visit the website below to make this book pop!

popbooksonline.com/dragons

*Scanning QR codes requires a web-enabled smart device with a QR code reader app and a camera.

TABLE OF CONTENTS

CHAPTER 1

DANGER IN THE DARK

Late at night, the village is quiet. The moon is high in the sky. People are sleeping. Suddenly, a thumping sound fills the air. Wings beat in the dark sky. A roar echoes over the village. A dragon is flying down from his mountain **lair**.

WATCH A VIDEO HERE!

Many dragons live in caves deep in the mountains.

Some dragons can breathe ice or steam instead of fire.

The villagers run to the forest to hide. Moments later, the dragon swoops through the streets. He lands in the town square. The ground shakes with his weight. Smoke rises from his nostrils. Fire streams from his mouth. Houses and barns burst into flames.

DID YOU KNOW?

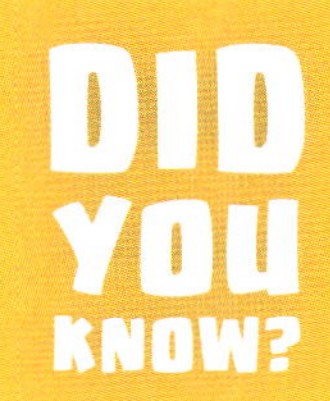

The name *dragon* comes from a Latin word that means "large snake."

The dragon roars again. Then he pumps his wings and flies back to his lair.

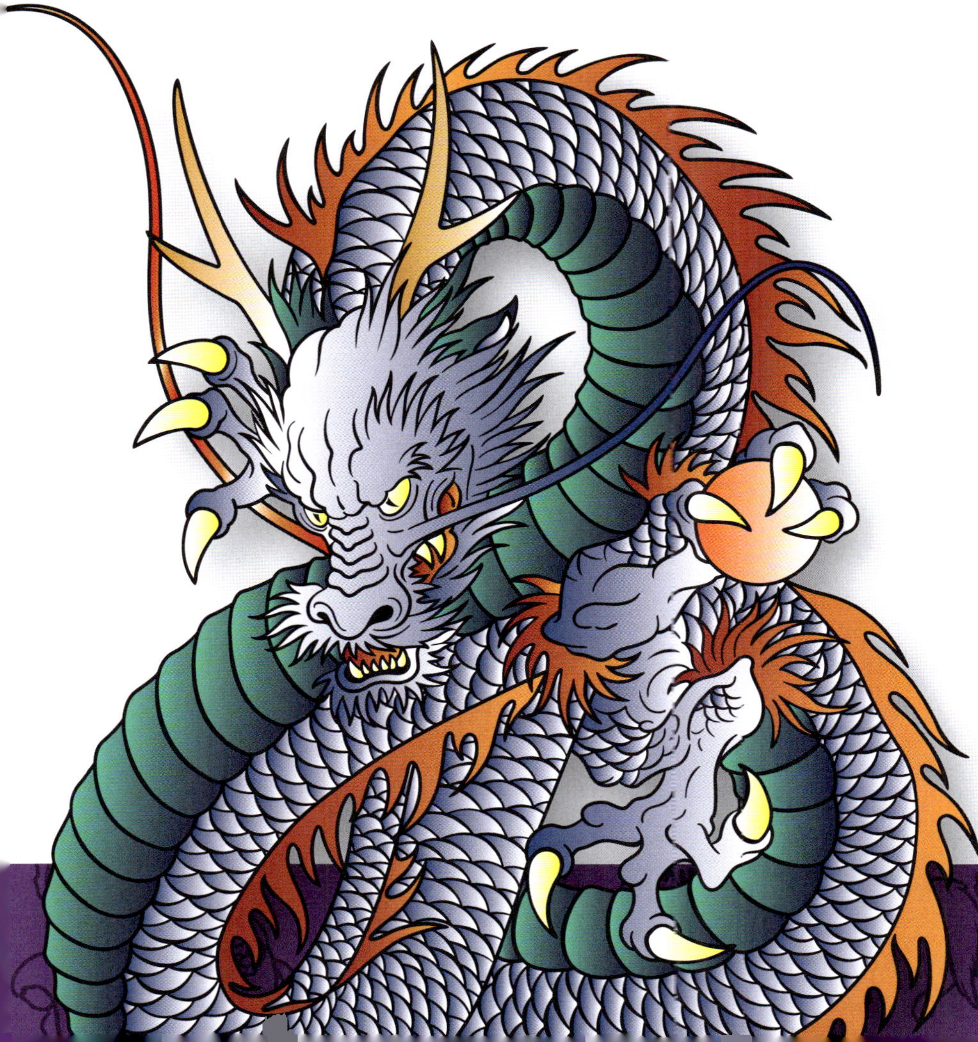

CHAPTER 2

DIFFERENT DRAGONS

Stories of dragons are everywhere. In fact, almost every **culture** in the world talks about a dragon-like creature. Each culture's dragon has different **traits**. But stories from similar parts of the world often have things in common.

LEARN MORE HERE!

Stories of dragons may have been inspired by whale bones that washed to shore.

In many Western legends, evil dragons attack people.

Most dragons in Western cultures are dangerous. Western cultures include people who live in Europe. People told stories of evil, fire-breathing dragons. The dragons hunted farm animals and destroyed villages. Some even kidnapped princesses.

In contrast, Eastern cultures see dragons as helpful. Eastern cultures come from countries in Asia. In their stories, dragons provide luck and knowledge. In fact, some people in China and Japan **worshipped** dragons. They believed dragons were gods.

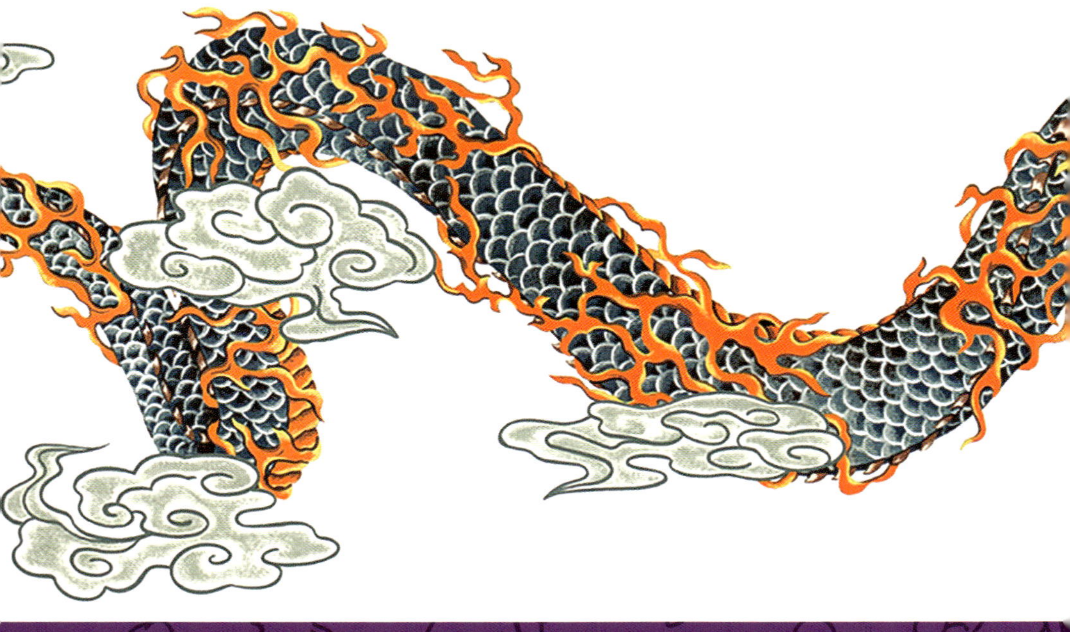

DID YOU KNOW?

The Japanese word for seahorse means "dragon's child." **Legends** said that seahorses were orphaned dragon babies.

Scientists agree that it is impossible for animals to breathe fire.

At first, Western dragons looked similar to snakes. But around 1000 CE, people in Europe told stories of a new kind of dragon. These dragons had

leathery wings and sharp horns. This **medieval** description of dragons is still common today.

Komodo dragons live on the island of Indonesia.

DRAGONS IN THE REAL WORLD

Many people believe stories of dragons are based on huge lizards and even dinosaurs. When people found dinosaur bones, they imagined a huge creature. Scientists think whale bones may have also inspired ancient legends of dragons. The closest creatures to dragons alive today are the Komodo dragons. Komodo dragons are the largest lizards on the planet.

DRAGONS THROUGH THE YEARS

4,500 BCE
People in ancient China carve images of dragons into jade.

800 CE
Vikings carve dragon heads into the front of their ships.

1400
A legend is written about Saint George saving a princess from an evil dragon.

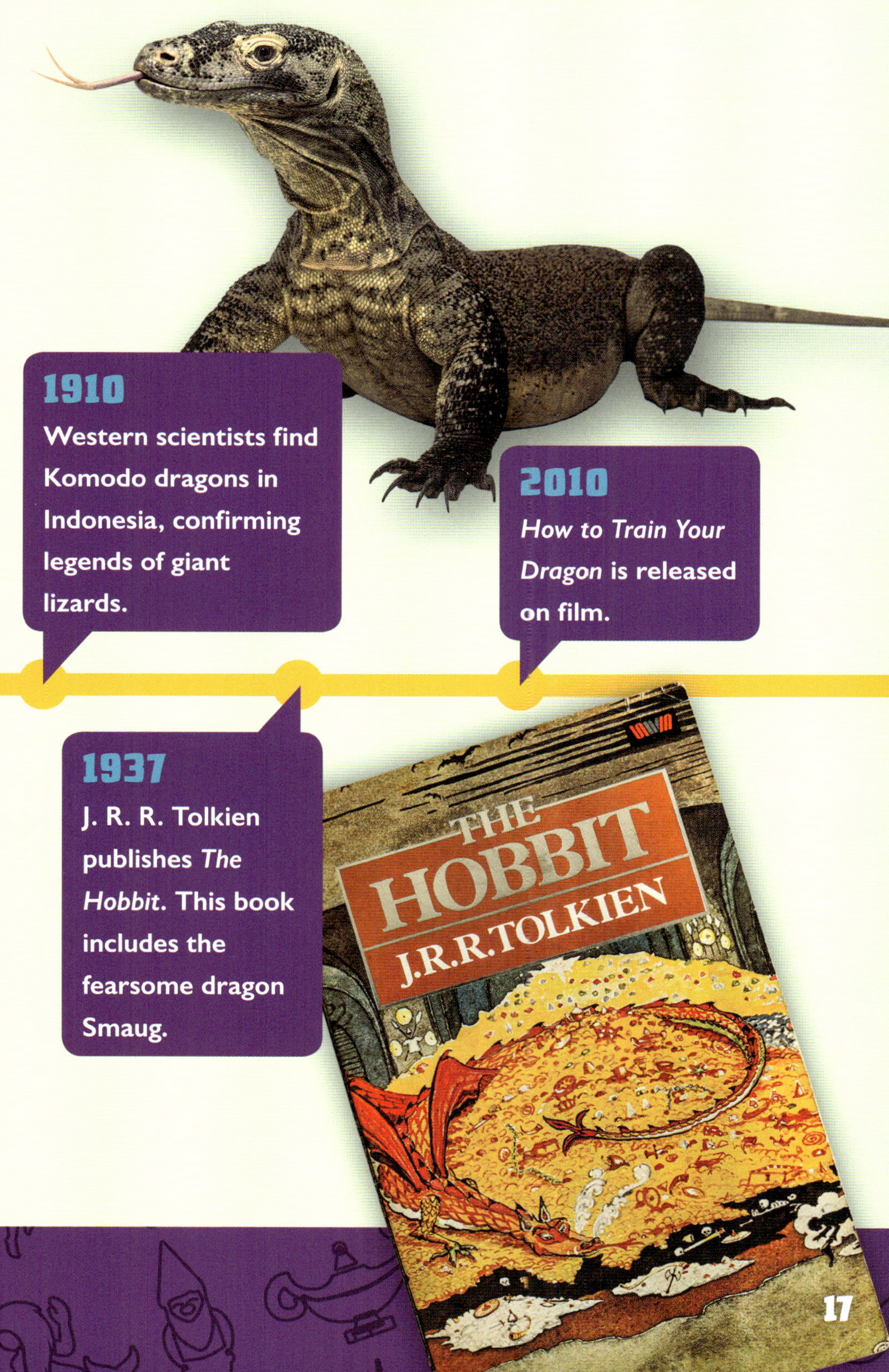

1910
Western scientists find Komodo dragons in Indonesia, confirming legends of giant lizards.

1937
J. R. R. Tolkien publishes *The Hobbit*. This book includes the fearsome dragon Smaug.

2010
How to Train Your Dragon is released on film.

CHAPTER 3
BUILT FOR FLIGHT

Many stories say dragons can fly. But not all dragons have wings. For example, Ryujin is a Japanese dragon that lives in the ocean. In stories, he looked like a sea snake.

COMPLETE AN ACTIVITY HERE!

Dragons that live in water sometimes have fins instead of wings.

Images of Eastern dragons can be found all over China and other Asian countries.

Dragons in Eastern **legends** have thick scales like a lizard. Eastern dragons have long bodies. They have four feet with sharp claws. Paintings show whiskers on their noses. These dragons do not have wings. They use magic to fly through the skies.

From 1889 to 1912, the Chinese flag featured a blue dragon.

Western dragons also have thick scales. But they are not as snake-like as Eastern dragons. Their wings look like a bat's. Western dragons have four legs with sharp claws. They have a long, powerful tail. They have sharp teeth and can breathe fire.

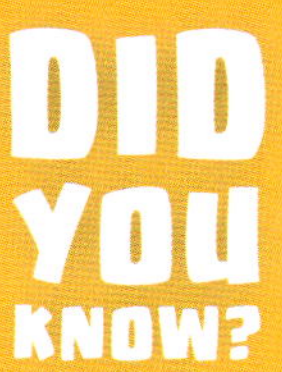

Today, dragons appear in TV shows and movies. Artists get ideas for how dragons look from bats, birds, and dinosaurs.

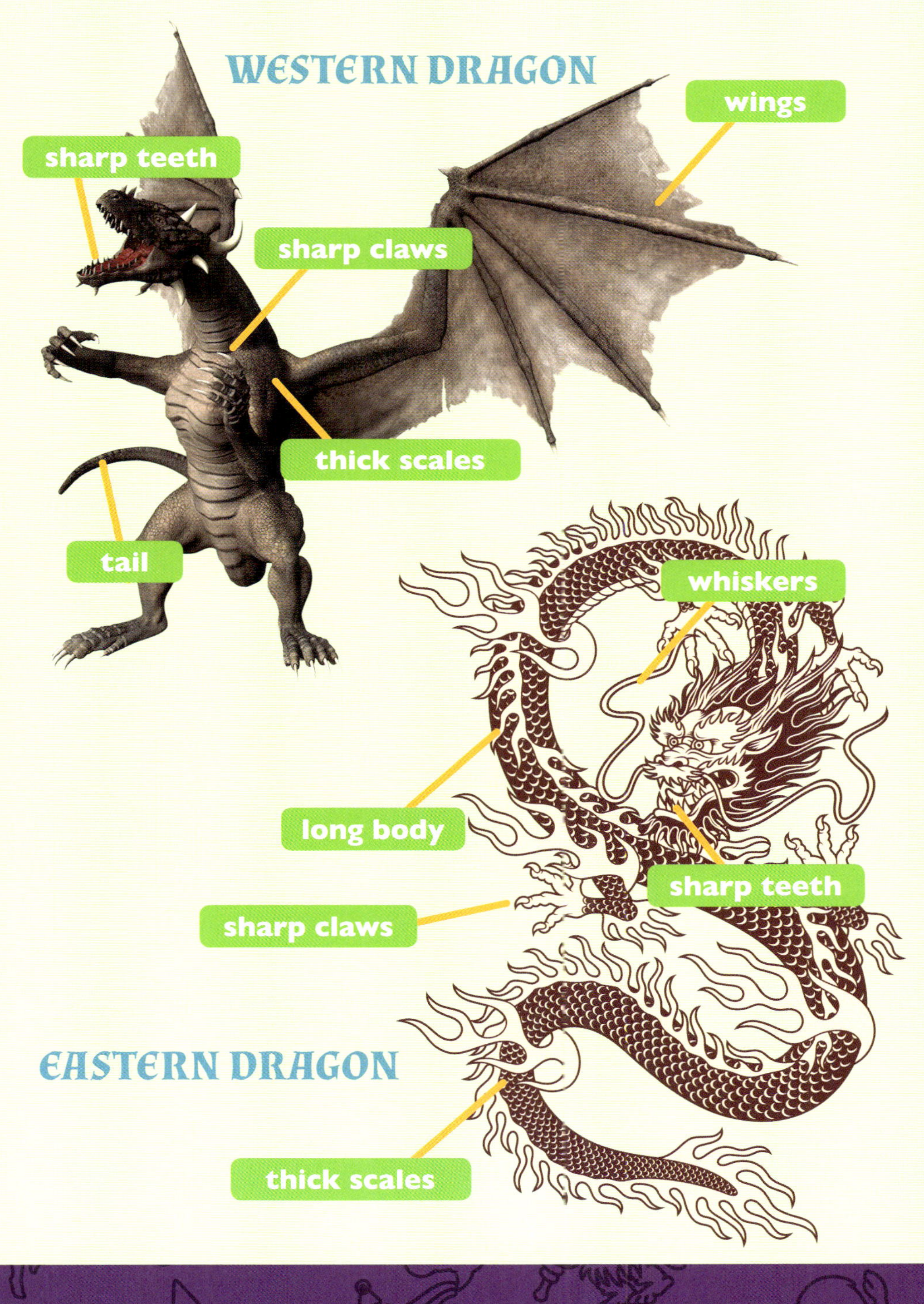
WESTERN DRAGON
sharp teeth
wings
sharp claws
thick scales
tail
whiskers
long body
sharp teeth
sharp claws
EASTERN DRAGON
thick scales

CHAPTER 4

PEOPLE AND DRAGONS

Dragons behave differently depending on the **culture**. Western **legends** warn that dragons are dangerous and deadly. They say dragons live in dark places.

LEARN MORE HERE!

Fighting a dragon often gave young knights a chance to prove themselves.

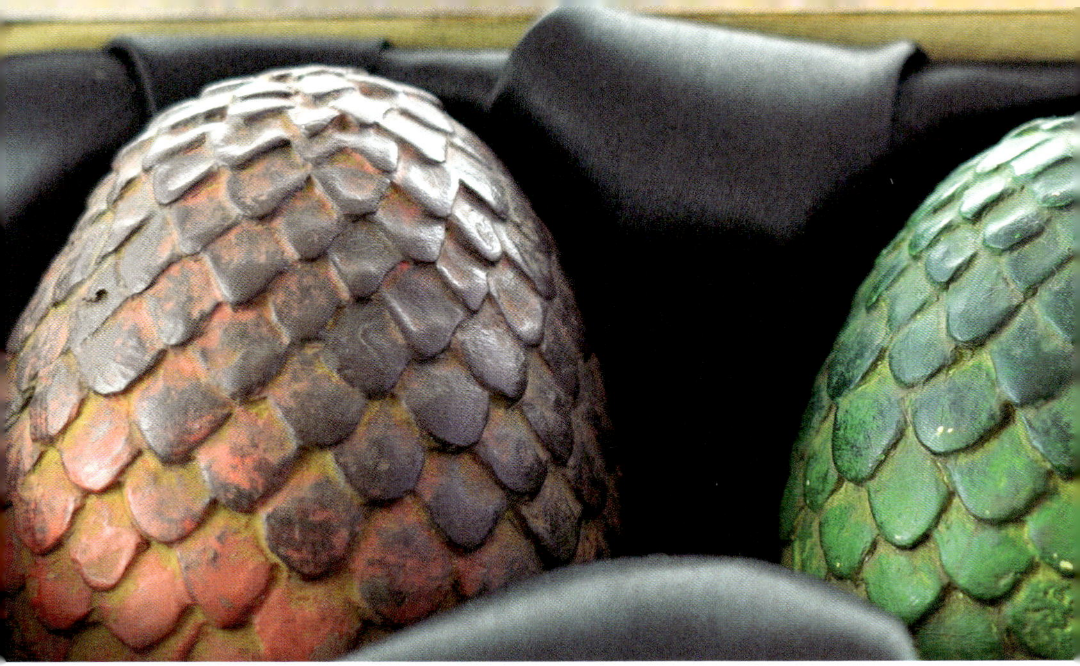

Western dragons live in caves or mountains. They often guard a **hoard** of treasure. Western dragons are greedy.

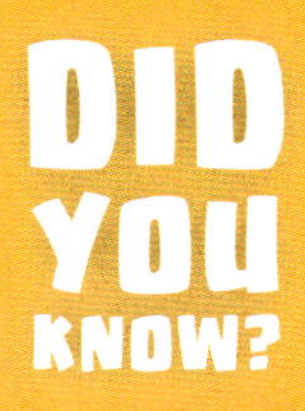

Some stories say dragons give people the power to see the future.

In many Western legends, dragons hatch from eggs.

If people try to take their treasure, the dragons will attack.

Western stories often talk about heroes who kill dragons. One example was Saint George. He killed a dragon to protect a princess.

In Eastern legends, dragons are often friendly and wise. They are very smart. Many stories tell of dragons helping people. In one story, a naga king kept the Buddha safe while he meditated. Nagas are snake-like dragons.

Eastern dragons are often connected to water. They live in lakes and rivers. They cause rains to come. Some legends say these dragons can change the seasons.

Today, this dragon bridge in Vietnam helps people cross a river.

MAKING CONNECTIONS

TEXT-TO-SELF

Are you more familiar with Eastern dragons or Western dragons?

TEXT-TO-TEXT

What other books have you read about dragons? What similarities or differences did you notice between those books and this one?

TEXT-TO-WORLD

Why do you think there are different descriptions of dragons? What do these descriptions say about each culture's values?

GLOSSARY

culture – the ideas, lifestyle, and traditions of a group of people.

hoard – a large collection of money or other valuable objects.

lair – the hiding place of a dragon.

legend – a story passed down over many years.

medieval – related to a time in European history from 500 CE to 1500 CE.

trait – the way something looks or acts.

worship – to honor or pray to a god or being.

INDEX

ONLINE RESOURCES

popbooksonline.com

Scan this code* and others like it while you read, or visit the website below to make this book pop!

popbooksonline.com/dragons

*Scanning QR codes requires a web-enabled smart device with a QR code reader app and a camera.